What Is Columbus Day?

By Margot Parker

Illustrated by Matt Bates

CHILDRENS PRESS ®

CHICAGO

Library of Congress Cataloging in Publication Data

Parker, Margot.
   What is Columbus Day?

   (Easy reading book)
   Summary: Explains the significance of Columbus
Day as a celebration of the first voyage made by
Christopher Columbus, during which he discovered
America.
   1.   Columbus Day—Juvenile literature.   2.   Columbus,
Christopher—Juvenile literature.   3.   America—Discovery
and exploration—Spanish—Juvenile literature.
[1.   Columbus Day.   2.   Columbus, Christopher.   3.   America
—Discovery and exploration—Spanish]   I.   Bates, Matt,
ill.   II.   Title.   III.   Series.
E120.P24   1985   970.1'5   85-12748
ISBN 0-516-03781-1   AACR2

"Hi, Amy!" said Ben.
"What are you doing?"

"Trying to figure out something,"
said Amy. "What is Columbus Day?"

"Well," Ben drew a deep breath, "Columbus was the man who discovered America. Columbus Day is the date when we remember it."

"You mean it's like my birthday?"
said Amy.

"Well, something like that,"
said Ben.

"Christopher Columbus
was an Italian who
explored for Spain,
hundreds and hundreds
of years ago.

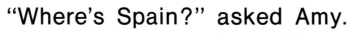

"Where's Spain?" asked Amy.
"Spain is on the other side
of the Atlantic Ocean,
hundreds and hundreds
of miles away.

UNITED
STATES

ATLANTIC
OCEAN

PORTUGAL

SPAIN

9

"Look, I'll show you—see
this globe," said Ben.

"Why is a globe round?" asked Amy.

"Because the world is round,"
said Ben, "But people
long ago ..."
"You mean hundreds
and hundreds of
years ago?" said Amy.

"Yes, Amy. Hundreds and hundreds of years ago some people thought the world was flat.

"They thought if they sailed
a ship too far, they would
come to the end of the
earth and drop off."

"What would happen if they
dropped off?" asked Amy.

"Well, they thought," said Ben,
"monsters would catch their ships
and eat them."

"You mean ships, men, and everything?" cried Amy.
"Yeah," said Ben.

"Is that true, Ben?"

"Nope," said Ben. "As I said, the world is really round, and if it is round, they couldn't fall off.

"Anyway, all Columbus really
wanted to do was to find a
faster way to the Indies."

"Oh," said Amy.
"What happened?
Did he do it?"

"Well, Columbus went to
the King and Queen of Spain
to ask for ships and money.
The King said 'No!'

"But Queen Isabella, who was beautiful and smart, said 'Yes!'

26

"She even offered to sell her
jewels so Columbus could go.

"She didn't have to, though.
Queen Isabella kept her jewels.

"Instead, the Treasurer of Spain
gave Columbus the money—
thousands and thousands of dollars!

"Then Queen Isabella gave
Columbus three ships.

"The *Santa Maria* was
the largest. It had a
crew of forty men.

"The two smaller ships were called the *Pinta,* which had a crew of twenty-six men,

and the *Niña,* which had a crew
of twenty-four men," said Ben.

"They had to cook on wood stoves," said Ben, "and had only compasses and the stars to show them the way."

"And they sailed and sailed
for hundreds and hundreds
of days," said Amy,

"and fell off the edge
of the world!"

"Nope," said Ben. "Only
thirty-six long days.
And they didn't sail off
the edge of the world,
Amy, because the world
is really round."

"Hurry," said Amy.
"What happened next?"

"They had a hard trip,"
said Ben. "Rough seas.

Bad food. The men on the
ship were sick and tired.

They had never sailed so long
without seeing land.

"But on October 12, 1492,
Columbus saw land. And before noon,
the ships landed on the beach
at Fernandez Bay.

"Christopher Columbus claimed the new land for Spain."

"So every October 12th
we celebrate Columbus Day,"
said Amy.
"Right," said Ben.

"I think I'll make a
picture for Columbus Day,"
said Amy. "Columbus
was a brave and
important person."

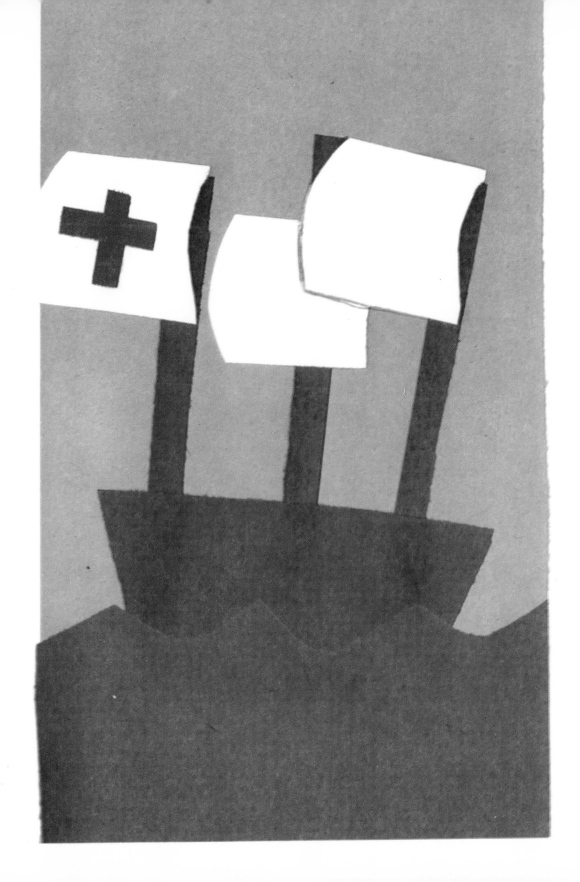

EPILOGUE

Christopher Columbus was a great seaman with one idea—to reach the Indies in the East by sailing West. He never reached the Indies (which at that time meant India, China, the East Indies, and Japan), because America got in the way. But he discovered a new continent, one that the people in Europe did not know even existed.

THE AUTHOR

Margot Parker has been a kindergarten teacher with Sacramento City Schools for more than twenty years. She is a graduate of California State University at Sacramento, is married, and has two grown children. Her search for illustrated books that explain why people celebrate special days prompted her to write this *What Is* series for young children.

THE ILLUSTRATOR

Matt Bates has studied art at Cosumnes River College in Sacramento and the California Institute of the Arts in Valencia. He also has studied under Louis Gadaul and with several Walt Disney animators, including Hal Ambro, T. Hee, and Bob McCrea. He is currently working as a staff artist with Marvel Productions in Van Nuys, California.